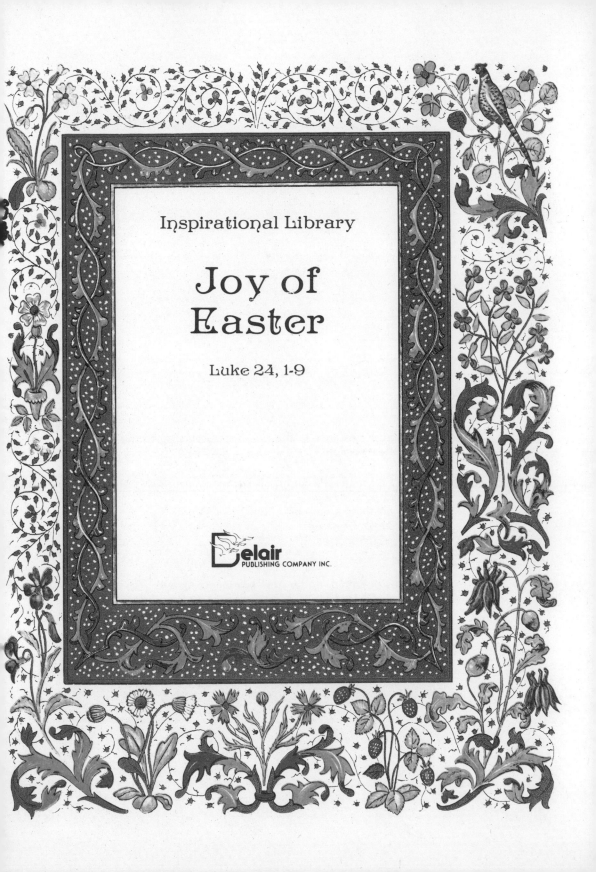

Inspirational Library

Joy of Easter

Luke 24, 1-9

Delair
PUBLISHING COMPANY INC.

All Scripture passages in this book are according to the
King James Version.

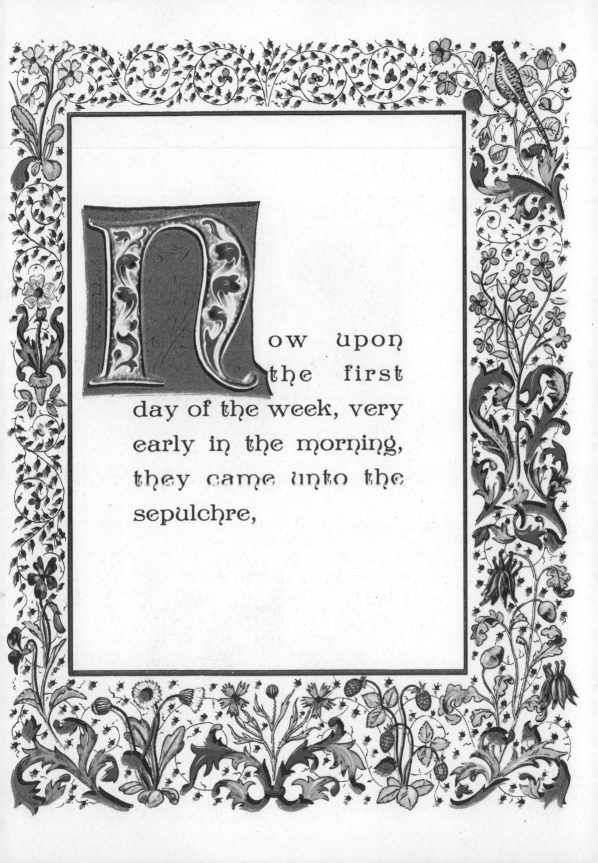

Now upon the first day of the week, very early in the morning, they came unto the sepulchre,

Bringing the spices which they had prepared, and certain others with them.

And they found the stone rolled away from the sepulchre.

nd they
entered in
and found not the body
of the Lord Jesus.

And it came
to pass, as
they were much
perplexed thereabout.

ehold, two
men stood
by them in shining
garments;

And as they were afraid, and bowed down their faces to the earth,

hey said unto them, Why seek ye the living among the dead?

e is not here,

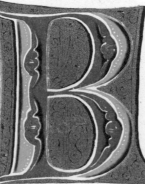ut is risen; remember how he spake unto you when he was yet in Galilee, Saying,

The Son of Man must be delivered into the hands of sinful men,

nd be crucified, and the third day rise again.

And they remembered his words,

And returned from the sepulchre, and told all these things unto the eleven, and to all the rest.